Newbie Author
This Chick's Journey to Becoming a Self-Published Author

By Carolynne Raymond

By Carolynne Raymond

NOVELS

The Crinkled Page

Titles available in The Earth & Airus Series

(in reading order):

A Life Cycle Reborn

A Life Again

NONFICTION

Newbie Author – This Chick's Journey to Becoming a
Self-Published Author

FOR CHILDREN

What Does Teddy Do While You Are Away All Day?

Newbie Author
This Chick's Journey to Becoming a Self-Published Author

By Carolynne Raymond

Newbie Author
This Chick's Journey to Becoming a Self-Published Author

By Carolynne Raymond

Introduction

Before this book was even an idea, I was writing and posting these blurbs on social media. The thought was to create monthly posts about writing. It wasn't just about documenting my journey to create a book even though that is what ended up happening. I smile because it sounds like I'm in denial, but really the first thing to understand when you are writing stories is you need to focus your time on what matters and for me, I didn't want to have to maintain a blog site but, in another breath, I wanted to track my journey. I did share my monthly blog posts on the mainstream social media sites as a way to make myself engage. Normally I'm that person who reads and scrolls and doesn't usually post anything but once I became an author and ultimately had a product to sell, engagement became a priority.

As these posts became regular in the beginning, I had doubts in myself on if I would be able to commit to a journal entry every month but month after month rolled by and I was able to commit to the entries and from there, I eventually started to use Wattpad to help put this writing journey all together and into this book.

A little bit about myself, I was born and raised in Ottawa, Canada. I have a younger brother and sister. I am married to someone who keeps my head out of the clouds and a son who keeps me on my toes. Writing has been a hobby of mine since 2012, and was realized in my thirties. What got me to eventually try writing was that from early childhood I always enjoyed stories. Stories brought worlds to life and sparks the imagination and from this love for stories it also sparked other creative outlets, like I enjoy photography, painting, and gardening. I also appreciate the work of others. When I am not working or playing with my son, you can find me curled up on the couch with a bowl of popcorn and watching anything from reality TV to fantasy, to science-fiction, to stories that are based on true events. I love thrillers, comedies you name it. I know it is a weird combination but please understand that I am a sucker for good laughs and also captivating stories.

Besides reading and writing I love to play video games, though I don't play much anymore because of the lack of time but I admit, I am a total nerd, I used to play World of Warcraft and I was a sucker for collecting the riding mounts in the game. When I am not reading or writing or being a couch potato, I walk; I also own a couple of kayaks and love to go out on the water. Swimming at my parent's camp and my parent in-law's retirement home is a must. I love to swim. This activity clears my mind and provides me time to think. It's whatever I decide to focus on.

Life at home is interesting. My husband and I are both Pisces and honestly, I think that if we had our own reality television show it would be a hit. I know I sound full of myself, but take what happened last week for instance. We had our front-end washer break. The first thing that happened was the clothes that were in the drum were trapped. I couldn't get the door to unlock so I gave up for a bit and then went back to it and to my amazement the door finally opened. I was like, yes! So, what do I do? I figured it was just a hiccup with the machine door locking up on me and I close the door again and re-run the load, when the rinse cycle came the machine stopped working again...

My husband tried his best to come to the rescue. He opens the back of it because at this point, we think there is a clog somewhere because the water isn't draining. He grabs hold of the water drain pipe, pulls it from the pump and then water comes gushing out, like really gushing out. He starts screaming at me, "What do I do?" I start getting the mop out but the water isn't slowing and after a moment of being silly I finally say, "Can you re-connect the hose to make the water stop?"

He does that and the water stops. We were tired, I blame fatigue for our lack of reason and after our basement flooded, we had to laugh and long story short, a repair man was contacted. Stories like this are the norm at our place.

I think the best way to describe my personality is that I am both shy and outgoing and I say this in one sentence. I am the type of person who struggles with starting up a conversation, I do force myself to and that is the shyness factor in me. I do have an outgoing side, I put things into action, I enjoy learning how to do stuff for myself and that is likely a huge factor as to why I decided to go through the self-publishing route. I enjoy seeing through a project from start to end. I published my first book, "A Life Cycle Reborn" on June 3, 2013. From six months leading to my published date and then afterwards, I learned a lot. I published more books and even dabbled in different genres, creating series, and writing standalone books.

You have chosen to read this book because you realize that there is so much more to becoming an author and it is not just about being able to write a story. Over the years I have written of my experiences and have compiled them together in order to share. These chapters follow a then and now layout, that cover my experiences back when I first started out as and author and my experiences now as an author all of these years later.

Chapter 1
One Month After Publishing My First Novel - Why Am I Not Famous?

Then…

I have to admit that as I edit this book, it is fun to look back on where my head was at shortly after publishing my first book. This adventure was only the beginning for me and back then I knew so little about all of it. This chapter provides insights to getting started and to paint a picture on how much your time is spread thin, leaving little time to market.

My novel, "A Life Cycle Reborn" has been available to the world for just over a month. I am a first-time author, editor, publisher and media person. I have hit some bumps along the way and I am still trying to figure out how to get around them.

The author part came easy because I loved storytelling and I had a story in my head for a while and it was just a matter of having it written. I am by no means a fancy writer and rely big time on spell check, Grammar Girl, Online Thesaurus, you get the picture!

The editing part was the beginning of this journey becoming harder. Reading what you have written, re-arranging thoughts, second guessing your use of grammar and allowing your hard work to be read by friends, family and complete strangers before it was ready and then bracing yourself for the criticism and all while trying your hardest to keep an open mind in order to make the necessary adjustments that your readers mentioned.

It was a lot and sometimes a good kick in the teeth because not every person will enjoy every part of your story and when I opened myself up to criticism and suggestion it sometimes discouraged and confused me because of the readers sharing new ideas that were not my own.

Publishing was sort of a little easier than editing, I say this because registering as a publisher was easy, and getting the ISBNs and copyright was straight forward. In Canada you can register yourself as a publisher in order to obtain free ISBNs and you can get a copyright for a small fee, mine cost $50.00 per publication. I did this by contacting the Canadian Federal Government. I searched for information on how to become a publisher, how to obtain ISBN's and copyrights and it led me to a government website ending in "gc.ca" I will let you do your own online search since web addresses sometimes change overtime. The federal government sites in Canada mostly end in☐gc.ca. If you are in another country which has their own websites, try searching a topic followed by naming your country and usually you will get local information. The "gc.ca" site has easy to understand instructions on how to get set up as a publisher and if you are unsure, inquiring with them directly is easy. I did this once with sending a question by email, through their "Contact Us" page and they answered within a day.

☐

Now…

☐

Since publishing my first book, ISBN's are getting much easier to obtain and I have learned that if you publish on some of the self-publishing sites, they will assign ISBNs to your books free of charge.

The hard part, for me was after doing all of the above and uploading the book to the retailer sites (which I will explain it in another chapter later on in this book) is you need to also set up your publisher profile with the retailers. Amazon owns a company called CreateSpace which was the print on demand site that eventually got absorbed into Amazon KDP and as a Canadian trying to create a print on demand book with an American retailer, they wanted me to fill out IRS tax forms and the thing is I didn't know how to get around this in order to proceed. What I didn't understand, is I was able to put my digital book on Amazon without filling out these tax forms, but with the print on demand, there was no way around it. For the time being, I had set aside the thought, I needed to learn more about it and I'll explain it more later on but essentially you want to complete those tax forms not only because you have to but because some countries have tax treaties with the United States and for Canadians we are exempt of the withholding tax.

Now for the fun part and I say this with sarcasm because hands down this is hard as hell to stay on top of even all of these years later. Being a media person, holy cow, this is bowsers. Once I published my book, I thought that because I am on all of the heavy hitter's sites, Amazon, Kobo, Barnes & Noble, and Apple that I would be receiving more activity, eyes viewing my books but that's not the case. The case is that you have to hustle. The truth is this book is just a tiny speck in the digital libraries around the world, and the hard thing is getting strangers to see that I actually exist. This is my challenge. Social Media is a start and I have been generating some activity on Facebook, Twitter and Pinterest, but from what I can see, my posts have sort of gone a little viral but they have puttered out shortly after. My biggest reach on one of my Facebook posts was 166,786 people (this was back in 2013 when you didn't have to pay for visibility) but the thing with that number is I believe it has to do with a person hitting "Like" on the post and then that "like" will show on that friends activity log, (the space on the right of your news feed) and the thing with that, is that the 166,786 Facebook users, I think is a potential max and not an actual max, not everyone is staring at the activity log when they are on Facebook.

I need to target my niche market but how and when do I have time to do this? I wrote an adventure, sci-fi, fantasy novel, there is a little adult content, but the feel it is young adult. I need to find those people who like these genres.

Now how to find them and get them to discover me!

Fast forward to present day and reading the blurb above you could see that I had taken on way too much at once. I was sprinting when I should have been tackling one thing at a time. That is part of the reason why my first book didn't shoot up the bestseller lists and put me front and center.

Today, writing, editing, marketing, publishing and managing the tax and business side of things is much more manageable. Some things like becoming a publisher is a one-time process, figuring out how to complete the tax forms is a one-time process. The retailer and publishing sites will have you refresh your tax details yearly but once that initial set up is complete your set and the only work is maintaining it yearly.

As I became more comfortable and confidant in my writing and storytelling by creating more novels, I cut out the steps of having readers review my transcripts. This isn't recommended by others who add their commentary online because typically having the added help is mostly beneficial but for me, having gone through this as an indie author I found it difficult to manage because everyone has their own opinions on how a story should go and I found that the advice sometimes took away from my initial ideas. Some advice was good, like one of my readers had suggested simpler character names, others had pointed out that some scenes were missing description of the surroundings, some pointed out grammar errors. I am thankful for their help and I am happy to have gone through the process on my first novel and have held onto some of the advice from those readers of my first novel and have applied their advice to my following books. For my latest book, "A Life Again" I knew the direction that I wanted to take the story in and I was much more confidant in my abilities and on top of that I found writing and editing tools are much more powerful. Like Microsoft word not only picks up on spelling and punctuation but they also pick up on poorly written sentences where the message isn't clear. Also, Word has a "text to speech feature" in its setting that you can add to your tool bar. I found this helpful because sometimes my eyes play tricks on me and I see what I meant to write, instead of what is actually written.

For marketing yourself and your books online, over the years I have noticed the gates close on visibility for free posts because social media sites want to monetize so unless you pay, you will not get much traction, however there are a few work arounds, it isn't imposable to get visibility. I have paid for some posts but I didn't see a positive impact other than increased traffic but it didn't increase my sales. This is likely because I still have not mastered targeting for paid posts meaning I am not clear on what time to post, how to reach my intended audience when building a paid post or how much I need to spend to make the paid post worth it.

For me I have manly stuck with maintaining a presence on social media. I followed those that I know are successful as authors and influencers and took notes on the kinds of posts they made and how frequent they posted on topics of marketing their own books versus posting about themselves and their lives. I also made an effort to engage in others posts. It's good to have followers but even now, I know that not all of them see my posts because for example my Facebook page has over five hundred followers however a post maybe gets on average 70 views. Anyway, I know the numbers seem bad but I am starting to see an upswing in page engagement because as I follow the lead of those who are successful and apply it to myself, I see my numbers have steadily increased in views and engagement. The most successful influencers don't try to blatantly sell to their viewers all the time. They may have a product captured in the background of a photo now and then, but for them they share about themselves, what they are doing, and the things that they love. They are social, and I believe that's why they do so well. I try to post every week about life, family, and my writing because that's comfortable for me. I make my posts casual and social and not like a marketing advertisement and I find those posts do the best. My landing pages have the links to my books and I am seeing an increase in profile clicks and sales. This is what works for me. Keep it casual, social, and maintain a post schedule, post your books every now and then but that's it. I keep it light.

Do what you can comfortably. Try not to get caught up in the details of social media because they are constantly changing. When you pick a platform to use in order to promote yourself, be present. Maintain a schedule that works for you, whether that's everyday or once a week, just be reliable for your audience.

Chapter 2
Two Months In – Reviews and Advice

Then...

☐

Pete and Repeat where in a boat, Pete jumped out, who was left? Ha, ha that's how I feel at this point, they say that the road to success is a long one, and I am starting to see it. So where am I at and how does this information help you? I will explain my progress so that you can gauge, what works, and what doesn't.

So far, I have more downloads to show and sales, not a lot, but I know I am making progress. I am waiting for my customers to take that brave leap and post a review. From the last update (these chapters used to be posted online where people could comment), I took the suggestion and purchased a couple of books on how to market for indie authors. I was able to apply some tips immediately, like adjusting book teasers to see if sales improve, other things I want to do is making a book movie trailer, and I just need to find time. There were a couple of things in the marketing books that I didn't agree with their ideas. Some books recommended using social media to promote yourself, which I do, but they said don't spam and I can see why, people tend to ignore it, but this is the thing that I am not sure on where I stand. For me ninety nine percent of the time, I personally ignore a spammer, but given a clever pitch, I may check them out. For myself, I tried spamming on twitter by sending maybe a hundred or so messages at a time to different people and out of those hundred I received a few downloads. On the other side of things, I have also reached out and had genuine conversations with twitter followers, this takes a bit more time and I will also get some results with this approach. I don't see a difference with the results, both generate about the same amount of results and I can see why spammers spam, it works, and it gets your name out there although it is super annoying to most on the receiving end and it is so time consuming as an indie author.

Since I have published I have taken an interest in social media and marketing and have gotten the approval from my boss at my real job to do some job shadowing of a professional who works in marketing, so who knows, I may switch career paths. Also, last month I was stumped with how to set up a CreateSpace print on demand book (CreateSpace is now Amazon KDP); I was stuck on not having a TIN because I'm not American. It turns out that I just need to complete a couple of forms which is supposed to be easy. Maybe on my post, "Three Months In" I may just have that print on demand book ready, and now to the juicy stuff!

Okay so through twitter, I learned of these groups of authors that read and review each other's books, I know that this is not a new concept. I joined a group, but am only watching the activity for now to get a better understanding of how these authors work. Well, I see that they post links to their work, some are free and some are not, but they all have one thing in common that they want a review and so they give reviews. Well, I took that bit of information and left it in the back of my mind. I'm not ready to participate.

Switching gears now, back to twitter. Within the last two weeks, I sent a direct message to a fellow author and pitched my book to them and they did the same. I know, you are asking where this is going; I am getting to the point. Here is where things took a turn for me. This person was so eager to get a review from me on any of his books that he was willing to go as far as send me, a stranger a personal PDF file of his work. My first thought is for myself, personally, I found it very difficult to do that with my own book, I did, but only with trusted people and the strangers that reviewed before I published were, friends of friends. For my own work I'm weary with giving away freebies. Now my second thought was if I said yes to him sending me a free book, what if this person ends up sending me a virus? And third let's say I agree to his free book, its virus free and I read it and it totally sucks, I agreed to a free book and he expects a review in trade! What did I do, I told him that, "I would rather support a fellow author with a purchase and for now I will download a sample from the retailer." He seemed happy with my response, sent me a couple of links to his books that he thought I would like and we ended the conversation. This was about two weeks ago. Since then, I have downloaded one of his samples, read it and fast forward to the present, I purchased the full copy for $5.00. I messaged him to say that I purchased and he returned the favor and purchased my own. So now I'm at the point where I liked his sample and am eager to get into his book and write a review for him and hope that he reviews mine.

Now here is my thinking, Authors want reviews because reviews are important, they help customers decide. I have been reading about writing styles, authors, and marketing for a year now and not once did I come across information of authors essentially buying each other's books to review. I will write a review because I said that I would and hope he returns the favor, but if he or I don't write each other a review, at the end of the day, in a small way, we helped each other with sales rank. I am not sure why a purchase for a purchase isn't talked about in the author world? Maybe this is assumed to be common knowledge? Maybe, I am not the sharpest knife in the drawer? It's like it's a taboo subject and I say that it shouldn't be because at the end of the day we are two readers who stumbled upon two great books and we are both motivated to support an author because we take pride in our purchase. These are my thoughts and findings so far.

Now…

Fast forward some years now and I can tell you that my thoughts mentioned above have changed for almost everything I had done back when I was starting out. Spamming, yes back then I admit to trying this and it generated sales but I advise against it. It is so incredibly time consuming, and today you run the risk of having social media accounts suspended if you have been flagged and besides, you can just focus on more productive things and free your time for things that you prefer to focus on. Marketing on social media today has pivoted greatly, a normal post will only generate a fraction of organic views then it did back in 2013 so now, the focus is paid ads. I have since tried running Facebook ads which generate a ton of views but the hurdle for me is that I need to learn how to target my ads and that takes time with learning how. Facebook does have resources for marketers but I admit that I took a step back and instead focused my own paid marketing with using Amazon ads. With Amazon ads their machine is finer tuned to those who don't know a thing about marketing and when setting up a paid ad, Amazon only asks a handful of questions and their machine will make all the adjustments to insure the success of your ad and I find that it respects the money you spend with them. For me I'll likely stick with Amazon ads as well as try other distributor ads as I branch out with paid marketing. When I had started out in 2013 I was against spending any money on paid ads because with the social media sites an unpaid post typically generated a lot of views but today it's not likely the case. I consider myself new to paid marketing but I realize now just how important it is to invest back into your business in being an author and selling books. Marketing is the key to getting discovered, and at least with today you do not need tons of money to run a paid add. You can run an ad for as little as a cup of coffee and I think that's amazing because it allows us indies to experiment and see what works and what doesn't. I'm excited to try the marketing options offered by other distributors and I feel like it's the distributors that I want to focus more on. I've yet to try twitter, instagram and other social media paid ads. I'll try them just to see but trying facebook paid ads didn't convert views to sales so I'm a little turned off by the experience but I do realize that facebook is one social media site so I'll give the others a try.

Today I don't seek out reviews the way I did back when I had fist started. You can try to encourage reviews through books swaps with other authors but you can run into problems. If you are doing a book swap, you are committed to reading a book that may not be your first choice and may feel pressure to write a more favorable review. You are also taking time away from yourself in committing to other things besides writing and being present in your own activities. In the handful of times that I had participated in a book swap with a fellow author I was lucky in that I truly enjoyed their books. I stopped participating in this because it is a huge commitment when you could be doing more constructive things with your time and I no longer participate. I do still write reviews for novels I have enjoyed but it is just me reading a book that I pick and when you read for leisure you can write a review in your own time and not be confined to writing a review on a short time table.

Reviews are important because they are in a way confirmation of approval for potential buyers and as long as you are active on the platforms you have chosen to connect with your readers, reviews will come. Instead of participating in book swaps to obtain reviews what I do now is at the end of each novel that I write I encourage my readers to provide a review. For me this takes minimal effort in that you only need to input that blurb once at the end of your novel. Also, when I come out with a new book, prior to the publish date I have found that offering my ARC, advanced reader copy to followers of my social media pages that helps too because you are giving early access to your fans without charging them. People that you have a connection and you gift them a story generally want to support you and return the favor in some way so they sometimes return the favor with a review.

Reviews take time. As you guessed it I'm no longer nervous with sharing my work like I had been when I was a newbie author.

I'm still one person doing many things so understanding that now, I have learned not to put pressure on myself to complete multiple tasks at once. You need to pick what matters most and work on it while protecting your time.

I focus on one step at a time and don't give myself tight deadlines. Like, if I want to film a video to promote my book, in order to help generate a review, I won't race to do it all in one day, I'll spread out filming and editing and posting the video over the course of a week or two because it's manageable for me. The thing for me is that my goal each day is to move the work forward in some way big or small. Like right now I'm working on a children's book and my goal is to take one picture a day with the intent of editing the photo to make it look like an illustration but for me as long as I do something to move the work forward it's a win. I could write a couple of sentences or a couple of pages and the win is that I did something. That mindset keeps me in a positive frame of mind because we all know how massive writing a book is, it's a lofty goal and looking at that ultimate goal with all of the work ahead of you can be scary and discouraging but breaking it down into small to do things is easy and manageable.

Chapter 3
Three Months In – Automatic Momentum

Then…

☐

Things are moving at a steady flow which is good. Today, I even had a couple people approach me in the hall at work to say that they started reading my book! I think that I am still wet behind the ears and I am at the point where I don't have that automatic momentum. What I mean by this, is I need to be constantly working to promote myself. I have noticed, that if I don't continue the effort and instead start to slack, my downloads and sales reflect my effort, so I know that I still haven't caught on yet (meaning that others are not yet talking about my book through the magic of word of mouth. This is my ultimate goal)

In my previous chapter, "Two Months In – Reviews and Advice" I talked about connecting with other authors and buying their books and they purchased mine in return in order to help with sales rank and obtain some reviews. I did that with a fellow author, I purchased his and he purchased mine. I read his work and enjoyed the novel and wrote a review, but he never provided me one. What I found out after I finished his work is and it's sad to say he looks to have given up on actively working on his own marketing and promotion. I checked out his twitter account to message him and say "Hey, I finished your book and loved it and posted a review!" He never got back to me and actually his twitter feed showed a post only days earlier basically implying that he had given up. It's sad and I am not sure what happened?

I know that I missed him by only a few days. I have learned that marketing and promoting your work is an upwards battle and that you really have to work at it to get noticed especially when there are tons of books.

My message to new or aspiring authors is please understand that this process is a long one, a labor of love and once you publish, you need to make the effort to have your book get noticed. This is my advice; keep at it because it takes time!

Changing subjects now, I still haven't created my print book! UGGG I know, you are screaming "BOOO!!!" I honestly gave it a fair shake. I had been looking at CreateSpace (Now Amazon KDP) for a couple of months now, and decided that I would do something different and take a look at one of CreateSpace's competitors (Createspace is now KDP). I went through all the steps and arrived on the pricing page and was so disappointed! I have read articles that say, "If you have nothing nice to say, don't say anything..." and maybe I'm putting my foot in my mouth, but I have to say it because I was really upset. For me to make a profit with this other print on demand publisher, I needed to set my price at $25.00 to generate a few dollars from every distribution channel. I didn't like that at all, and it's not that I don't believe my book is worth it, trust me, I think I wrote a pretty good book, but let's face it most paperback novels are set at the $9.99 price mark. That is what I wanted to set mine at, but if I did that, I would have left myself out of the payment pie.

I am going to have to keep looking for a good print on demand place that allows self-published authors create a great print on demand book that is also priced fairly, but first, I need a TIN to go further and I need that extra push of confidence to do it.

My last topic is my second book. I am making progress and am totally enjoying it. I am not close to being completed my first draft but I am getting there, can't wait to be done!

Now...

☐

Automatic momentum is like trying to find the end of a rainbow. Years later and I still haven't achieved this, however I think I have achieved steady momentum. I have regular sales but not the amount that would launch me to a bestseller's list. I think the reasons for the automatic momentum not working out for me are a few things. First would be, I have stayed away from paid advertisements and I think paying for ads would increase my reach and help me build momentum. I haven't networked in person at local bookstores and book groups. The opportunities are within reach but I have not given that a try and another thing is I think that I need to create more books. I say this because since publishing my sequel, "A Life Again" I have found that by default my first book, "A Life Cycle Reborn" also gains an increase in sales. This tells me that I need to keep coming up with new books because it not only provides another product to sell it also shines a light on my older products.

I believe automatic momentum exists because things go viral and without helping momentum along with money or a ton of effort in being on social media, automatic momentum is part luck and part strategy because you have to have a few things fall into place like, timing, the right eyes and the right appeal. I haven't had that combination. Today paperback novels average anywhere between $10 to $22 dollars and the following print presses allow for indie authors to publish paperbacks well within those price ranges and gives indie authors enough of a margin to generate royalties without added markups. Indie Authors can price their paperbacks competitively.

For my print on demand I ended up choosing Amazon KDP and Barnes and Noble and for my ebooks I use Smashwords, Amazon KDP and Drafts2Digital. For the print books the retail price point was important to me and Amazon KDP provides that good price point where I can compete with the price points of other great books and I was happy with the quality of the paperbacks. The set up of creating your paperback through both are very easy too because they have a ton of templates you can work with for the text and the templates are all formatted to allow headers, footers, and the page margins are all set up to account for the spine of the book. Creating a cover is easy too, they have templates that you can use to set your own images onto or you can use their cover creator tool if you don't have a cover created yet.

I never did hear back from that author that I talked about above in this chapter and I could have been ghosted by them but I don't think I was. I think they gave up. Marketing can be hard if you are not sure what you are doing and discouraging if you aren't seeing results but for the things that aren't working the sooner you can figure that out the sooner you can move onto trying something different. I'm not mainstream and I know what I have tried and learned what doesn't work and it can be frustrating when you are working with few resources but you have to ask yourself why you are doing this and for me writing brings me happiness and a sense of accomplishment. I started this because I love to write and create and when I do publish my work, I gain the sense of accomplishment from all those hours that I put into creating a novel. If you are not getting any joy from this then you need to step back and figure out why and once you figure that out you can move forward.

I know for myself; I have focused my time back into my writing and cutting back on time spent on social media, only committing to a post a week. I don't try to seek out reviews the way I did when I first started with book swaps but instead focus on being present and engaging when I am online as well as maintain my book links on my social media pages. I ignore negativity, although it can be hard when it's a message directed to you but when this happens, I found that for myself its best just to refrain from engaging all together. I have seen others react to negativity and it can go bad quickly. There are also tools on social media to block and report abuse. Don't be afraid to use them. Also, a lot of social media sites give you the option to just delete the negative comment.

Also, something that I haven't really committed a ton of time into is book contests. I have done some and it has gained me readers and some momentum all while continuing to focus on writing. Book contests do give your books visibility. Wattpad runs a lot of them and one of my goals is to enter into more of their contests because they have such an amazing reader base. Even if you don't win their contest you still win because your book is being showcased. When a book wins the contest, this launches the author and their books into that Automatic

Momentum, its not uncommon for them to get a ton of reads. Its amazing to see that there are free resources that can provide this without having to pay for visibility.

This past year I had participated in the Wattpad's annual Wattys and it was all around a good experience and they have resources for participants to refine their book blurb and pitch so even if you don't win the contest you win with refining your craft and coming up with good ways to pitch a novel for when you really are ready to publish.

Chapter 4
Four Months In – Social Media Peeps

Then...

I want to take a different route and talk more about the social media side of things. When I look at my numbers, I have over, 7600 followers on Twitter, over 2600 followers on Pinterest and over 500 followers on Facebook. My numbers grow daily which is just amazing and with those numbers I get to see into different lives that I would never encounter in my normal everyday life and as cheesy as it sounds, I feel so lucky that these strangers share with me a little about them.

For myself, I am a Canadian and I have lived in the Ottawa area my entire life. In my spare time have taken up writing. I don't travel often but when I have, I have visited other parts of Canada and the United States.

When I started these social media accounts, I had no idea the amount of traffic I would receive or the fact that my eyes would soon be opened to many other different, exciting and captivating, lives. I knew of the places where these people were from, but I didn't feel a connection to and now I can say different.

I talked to someone from Japan and they showed me the world through their eyes. They were color blind, but painted the most colorful paintings I have ever seen. Just beautiful, and the discipline in this person's art was truly breathtaking. They never had to share these images with me but they did and I got to see a form of art that isn't in any of the galleries here.

I talked to a professional boxer; I know! I couldn't believe he even struck up a conversation with me after I sent him a simple hello. He explained his passion for the sport and in talking to him learning that he was fearless in the ring. I asked if he was ever worried about getting hurt because I am a big chicken myself and the truth is, we are only given one body in this life. He told me, "Precisely and that's why I make the most of it, exercise, stay fit." That was his world and he couldn't refuse his passion for the sport because we all need to make the most of our lives and do what makes us happy.

I met an older woman in Great Britain. She has a name I have never heard of before and it sounds beautiful. Her home is near London and she sees a world of history and royalty. She is passionate about her home and its people, her pride shines through from the keyboard and her manors are well, they are better than my own. That's one thing that I have become more sensitive to is that typing conversations out shows no emotion so you have to be mindful because different dialects may take insult to something that you say that was intended to be friendly.

A girl from Australia showed me her world. She is probably one of the most positive people that I have ever spoken to and every photo I have seen of her, she looks truly happy. She lives in some sort of high-rise building and it blows my mind because she has wild parrots that visit her window for food. Colorful birds that I have only ever seen caged here in pet shops, but where she is these birds are free and they are also friendly looking creatures, I would have never thought and now I want to visit Australia.

Jumping a little north to India, I spoke to a young man who explained that he just purchased his first car and was a little anxious to start driving because the streets of India are well, crazy with elephants and cows walking free, millions of people, that was his world. Just like the woman I mentioned from Great Britain, this young man was also passionate about his country. He described it as exotic and full of history. I sort of had a sense of India from watching the Discovery Channel but this young man told it through his own eyes, an opposite world from where I live. Canada has less people than India.

I believe that humor is a universal language. I spoke to a hairdresser in Cuba recently and her humor quickly shown through. I told her that my own hairdresser knows pretty well everything about me and said she must hear a lot of interesting conversations while cutting hair. She explained that she knew where all the bodies were buried.

These are just six lives that I have described. Lives and worlds that I never really thought of but I do now. I think about these people and wonder if we will ever cross paths at some point. We take for granted being able to see people, hear their voices. I am sure that all of you that read this all see people in your own day to day lives, and these six never needed to share with me, they did and because of them I have learned more than I could have ever asked for.

Now...

In previous chapters I described taking a step back from social media to focus more on writing and unfortunately that comes at a cost and in this case, I miss out on meeting new people online. I think it is important to be open to meeting others because what they share can open your eyes to new things. There is a balance and it is a challenge. I admit that it is sometimes hard to remain open because I think these days direct messaging a stranger can be taken as intrusive and on top of that some of the direct messages I have received are those looking for love so naturally a wall goes up whenever a direct message is received from a stranger. I also find that with Instagram and Facebook conversations are kept light. People seem to refrain from getting into deep conversation and I don't think it is fear driving it but I think it is just become the norm we connect but it is shallow. There are some accounts that go against the norm, like "Humans of New York" They post pictures of people and there is a short but deep story about that person. It's still not the same as having a more direct conversation with a someone.

I have maintained relationships online with those I have met through writing, but I haven't branched out like I used to. There are options available like joining online groups, engaging more in other people's content and creating more of your own content. There is a balance of managing time between engagement and creation.

social networking online isn't hard but again it takes time and as an indie you have to be comfortable with the time you put into something. Do you want to spend your time networking online or is your time better spent in downtime growing your relationship with your family? □

Personally I have chosen my family and mastering my craft and it's the right thing for me. I set limits online which does limit the ability to network but with time there never is enough of it when yiu are trying to do as much as you can.

If you can afford to find others to help with aspects of your writing. Can you trust someone to run your social media? Maybe hire someone to help with edits or proof reading or design. Maybe someone can help with managing paid ad campaigns? Those are all of the things that take up my time. Right now its still just me working at it and in a day I may cover one to two things, like today I chose photographs to use in the creation of my next book and organized them into one folder on my laptop to edit later and I logged into my amazon paid ads and adjusted some of the targeting to try and improve my analytics and I edited this chapter, that was it.

Social media for me today is still a value. I have not deleted my accounts because social media reveals the trends, it shows you what others are interested in and its a platform to create presence, but I'm finding its not worth while to spend tons of time online because of the feeling of it being more shallow then it once was at least it feels that way for me. I know my experiences will differ from others and the takeaway from reading this chapter is to be conscious of the time you spend. Are you getting some sort of return from you time spent on social media sites? Are your friendships a value to you? Do you get something out of socializing like real friendships, shared learning through conversations with others? Are you building a following and gaining notice? You need to consider these things and reflect on whether what you are doing is working for you in some way and if it isn't then you know what to do.

Chapter 5
Five Months In – Getting Paid!

Then…

This past month things are coming into action. For starters, I officially received my first payment from Smashwords book sales, WOOT! I admit, I was getting worried because if you look at my time line from when I published my book, (June 3, 2013) I didn't see my first pay until the end of October. It makes sense now looking back on it because Smashwords pays quarterly and then they tack on an extra 30 days after the quarter is done. They explain this in the fine print of the contract. So, I just want to tell the Newbie Authors who may be anxious about the entire payment thing, it takes time, and Smashwords is upfront with your sales. They have a fantastic dashboard that tracks your book downloads and at the end of the day they come through for you!

Second thing, I am a friggen procrastinator! Somebody please kick me in the butt! I still haven't gotten the EIN thing set up for print on demand. Amazon and Smashwords, where I have chosen to sell my novel are based in the USA, so if you don't set up an EIN, the IRS withholds a percentage of your earnings and this applies to anybody who is not an American citizen. So far, I have loaded up a Skype account to make the telephone call to the IRS, but I have yet to call. I will do it soon, I promise!

Third thing is that I've decided that for now, I will hold off on the print on demand publishing. I think that for me the timing isn't right and I am basing that on gut instincts, I just don't feel comfortable with the idea and need more time to warm up to it.

Last thing, is Smashwords and Kindle introduced some new sales methods and channels which has gotten me curious. I have shared a couple of links on my Facebook page. I am going to check them out and see if this is something that I want to get on board with because let's face it, more options create more opportunities!

Now...

When I publish novels now, I publish both the e-book and the paperback at the same time. I use Amazon, Smashwords, and Draft2Digital for the e-book and Amazon and Barnes and Noble for the paperback and creating the paperback is a smooth process because for both they have set up the process to make it easy to convert your e-book to a paperback so it is a bit of an afterthought.

Getting paid today isn't a worry anymore because I have been using Amazon and Smashwords for years and Draft2Digital I have been using for a couple of years. Amazon pays monthly while Smashwords and Drafts2Digital pay quarterly. I check my reports quarterly just to make sure amounts match the payments and that's about it. I don't spend a lot of time on it. These companies have really made this easy for indie authors to focus on their writing and not worry about sales, payments or even completing taxes. The only other thing that I may look at a sales report is to see if jumps in sales have any correlation with the social media posts that were published.

Getting paid will happen and since Indie publishing isn't a new concept there are so many resources authors can look to in order to adopt the latest trends and improve their earnings. The thing is that you need to be aware of the news for indies. Sign up to distributer emails, join indie author social media groups to learn the trends in what's working for fellow authors like you. Some authors even post their earnings analytics along with the things they did to achieve their sales.

Chapter 6
Six Months In – Got Some Reviews & Stepped into Action

Then...

I got hard on myself because I had to. I was being a bum and not doing what I needed to in order to benefit. I finally did what I had been putting off for a while, I registered for my EIN. Honestly, the entire process was much easier than I had thought and I was able to actually use tips learned from fellow authors.

I got a PayPal and a Skype account in order to put money towards the international call. I visited the IRS website and printed out the SS4 form. This is the form that is needed in order to get an EIN number and I filled it out to the best of my knowledge. When I was on the call, the representative went through it with me. It was also good to have the form completed prior to the call because the representative went through the spelling of names, addresses and such and it is easier to see what you are spelling out to them when you have the form completed in front of you. When you speak to the IRS, they will introduce themselves and ask you the nature of your call and for me, a self-published Author, I said that I was calling for an EIN. From here on the representative guided the call, they are friendly and efficient and in hind sight it was silly of me to wait so long to do this.

My book is published through Smashwords and Amazon, those are both American companies and in order to not be taxed so heavily I needed the EIN, which I now have WOOT! With the two companies, when I logged into my author profiles with them, I had the option to fill out a W-8BEN form and I did this for both.

I received some more reviews on the Kobo and Amazon website and I love seeing that my book is being enjoyed. I have to tell you, it is funny because I am pretty bad at times with putting my foot in my mouth and spilling the beans and I have had some people send me an email while they were partway through the story, explaining that they think that something will happen next and all I can do is tell them that I am happy that they are reading because I would hate to spoil my own story.

So, what's next for this Author? Well, I am at the six-month mark of being published, so, I am not sure if I should still be called new, maybe I should upgrade my status to novice? Everything that I have set up to accomplish with this book is almost complete. The one thing left lingering on my "To Do" list is re-evaluating print on demand, which I plan to look at one more time before the year is through. Also, I lied, there is one other thing, and I want to have a look at making my story a recording. I had not considered this avenue before but a little bird mentioned it in passing, so I plan to look and see as the concept makes sense.

Now…

Reading this chapter and shaking my head. I was a dork to have waited so long in obtaining that EIN and really if you are reading this and you haven't gotten one but need to, honestly you don't need to procrastinate for six months like I did. It really is easy to do. The form is easy to complete and the longest thing to do would be maybe waiting to speak to someone from the IRS, which really didn't take long considering other things that I have waited on hold for in the past.

Hearing from readers always makes me smile and never gets dull, even all of these years later and its so cool when they volunteer to be test readers for your next work. Whenever you have that sort of engagement you know that you are doing something right. There isn't much more to say then that.

Creating print on demand paperback versions of my book has been one of the best decisions I have made when it comes to being an author. For one thing you have a product you can hold, how cool is that! You are appealing to a different crowd of people. Some people don't have e-readers or they just prefer reading a book over reading from a screen and you have a product you can use in promoting your work in the real world like participating in book signings, or giveaways or even just dropping off some copies in your neighborhood library box. On a side note there are now print on demand companies that offer hardcover novels which I totally want to do forever and today indies can do this without cost. Amazon KDP and Barnes & Noble offer this service for free and they are both amazing. I had created and purchased my own copies from both retailers and both companies truly create quality books. There are other distributors that offer hardcover options to indie authors at a small cost but I haven't worked with those companies because what kdp and B&N has, I'm satisfied with though the only reason that I may keep my eyes opened for other companies offering hardcover creation is for gaining a broader distribution but so far I haven't seen any other free hardcover creation services.

The other thing mentioned in the "Then" section was creating an audio book and I still haven't done this but I want to for the same reasons as creating a paperback and hardcover version in that you are appealing to other groups of people. The options now for creating an audiobook are much more easily available and the prices have come down over the years, so much so that Indie authors now have the option to do their own recordings and submit at no cost. Before, you had to hire one of their voice actors or actresses from the companies offering audio services, which could run you into spending hundreds of dollars and you have to arrange timelines that may differ from what your expectations are. I had looked into it all those years ago and decided to put it off because of the costs and to be honest I had forgotten about it.

I would prefer to do the audio myself to save on costs, and time to recruit and work with a voice actor and also for the reason that I know how my characters react in my stories, their level of emotions, their accents and their disposition and its easier for me to act that out then to direct an actor through the entire novel.

My plan is to soon to work with my dad in creating the audio as he has the professional recording equipment and has a general understanding in recording and reaching the levels you need in order to achieve a quality audio file. For me because I have family asa resource it makes more sense to do it this way but if you are somone who doesn't have access to the equipment needed to create a quality audio file then maybe hiring a voice actor makes the most sense. The take away from me writing about this is to know that you have both paid and free audio services available to you.

Just thinking about an audio version of my own books makes me smile and I can't wait to get started on this and learn this completely other side in publishing audio books and taping into a new market!

Chapter 7
Seven Months In – Now Considering Myself a Novice

Then…

As I write these words my mind is sort of elsewhere. I just realized that I misplaced something of value and for the life of me I can't remember where I hid it. My mind is always on the go, thinking about things, like plots, creating scenes, and writing chapters like this one and now when I want to find that valued item, I have no idea where I put it and it's driving me absolutely bonkers!

This is what I did in the last month regarding my book. For a while I have thought about doing a print on demand version of my book and played with the idea of taking that step-in previous months, but had always pulled away from the idea in the end for many reasons, such as, I was not happy with the rules, specifically the price point and wasn't happy with some of the sites forcing its users to pay for un-desired added services. Well, today I can say that I actually now have a print on demand version of my book, "A Life Cycle Reborn" and it was created with the help of a site called CreateSpace (Now Amazon KDP).

If you have already formatted your book for e-reader, creating your print on demand version can be done with ease. For me the hardest part was transferring my cover image to fit into one of CreateSpace's fixed templates. That took me time to figure out and come up with something that I was happy with. So, as I write this, I have already ordered my own print version of my book as a keepsake and am anxiously checking the mailbox every day.

What is next for me, I am just dying to figure out where I hid that thing, I have been trying to locate all night. As for the writing side of things, because I am in the middle of writing more books, I am now investigating a good text to speech software to use as a way to proof read and edit.

I have learned with writing, sometimes when you read things on a page you see what you intended to write instead of what is actually written on the page and with text to speech the voice says it exactly how it is written. Also, the nice thing with text to speech is it can help you with hearing where and where not to put a pause, such as a comma or a period. For now, on my iPhone I am trying out the free versions of iSpeech, and Natural Read. Anyway, that is all for this month and check in soon!

Now...

After reading the above I have no idea what I had misplaced but I can tell you that now that I'm older I misplace things all of the time! Passwords are my enemy even when I write them down I somehow enter them in wrong and lock myself out of apps, my phone. I've had to contact Apple because I completely forgot my passcode once. My toddler has this battery-operated ATV and I misplaced the charger. Like I completely turned the house upside down looking for this charger and never could find it but thankfully my spouse loves battery operated tools so I use one of his chargers, I think it belongs to a flashlight but it fits my son's ATV. I can keep writing about the things I lose but I won't. You get the picture.

Creating paperbacks and eventually hardcover versions of my books was totally worth it as I mentioned previously. Having different versions of your work just opens up the opportunity to reach readers who prefer certain formats. Today creating audiobooks is my new focus and it's a good spot to point out that if something isn't feasible now for whatever reasons, like cost, time or resources, it could change later on, which was what I encountered when looking into creating my own audiobook all those years ago and deciding not to proceed for a few reasons. Today the audiobook sites have cleared those bars of entry by removing the requirement of hiring voice actors. So, if something is a no go for you now, I'm here to say that it's okay and don't completely forget about it if its something you really want to do. The industry is constantly changing and if there are things in the way today, later on those things may go away, giving you the opportunity to move forward.

For the text to speech I have deleted the apps that I had been looking at because they ended up being redundant for me. If you have a word document software chances are there is text to speech within the software that you just need to add to your toolbar or its possible that the software is already there within your main menus. I use Microsoft Word and within the software is called "Read Aloud" found in the "Review" tab. I live this feature because even after years of writing and editing and proofreading it's been so useful to me to stop looking at the pages and simply listen to what is written.

It's amazing how much errors will stand out when you have a voice speaking the words to you.

So, you have learned that if you are forgetful, try to come up with a method to help you remember. I do write things down but not all the time or I'll write it down wrong so I have to be more sensitive to that. A no go today may turn into a yes go tomorrow so don't give up on an idea if that is something that you want to do and text to speech is amazing and word applications get more powerful as the years pass. The are always coming out with new and innovative features. For me if I'm looking for something that I want to do with my documents, I'll enter the question into my browser to see what resources can give me what I want and chances are, you have those features within your existing apps but if not, searching also can introduce you to new apps that do all sorts of other things that you never even considered.

Chapter 8
Eight Months In – Work & Results

Then…

Another month rolls on by and here is where I'm at. I found the thing that I had lost last month and learned that I shouldn't hide stuff because I have the memory of a squirrel.

I received the first copy of my print on demand book. I never ever thought that it would be as important to me as it was. I have to admit that I did shed some tears at actually seeing my work in its real form; too cool is all I can say and I am completely happy that I didn't give up on searching for a way that felt right for me.

On a second note, I made a really short video for social media to show everyone my actual book. To my surprise, the video received over eight hundred unique views. I also entered my very first writing competition, the outcome of it won't be revealed until many months later and I'm glad that I took the time to enter and the fun thing about being in the new year is I have picked up on the fact that this seems to be the season for contests and competition as I have learned of a few and I plan to jump on each opportunity. I figure why not right? The hard part of writing a book is over and all it is now is pretty much throwing your name into the draw and not to mention some of the prizes are worth the effort. So, my advice is to keep your eyes peeled. I recommend for the indie writers to log onto your distributer's websites, chances are there is a contest waiting for your submission.

Now switching over to software stuff, last month I had talked briefly about text to speech software. I have tried out a couple on my phone and computer and found that the one that I liked the most was Natural Reader for the pc. The software can handle a full-length novel and the free voice is good and you also have the ability to slow or speed up the voice. The application for iPhone is good, but there are limitations in how many words you can enter into it and if you load too much, the application will stop working and produce an error. So, for me, I have yet to find an alternative for my phone but give the Natural Reader pc version my approval and plan to use it to assist in editing.

So now what do I do? Well right now, I am working on my next books, I have one written and in the editing stage, I have a second that I am just over forty thousand words written and a third where the storyline is complete. Also, since having produced my print on demand version of my book I sent two copies to Library & Archives Canada, I will be mailing that out this week and lastly, I will be working on a submission to a second competition this week for, "A Life Cycle Reborn".

Now...

Good advice is don't hide stuff, even if you are sure that you will remember or even if you think it's the best hiding spot or that it makes the most sense because chances are you will forget. If you must hide something, I recommend that you take note of where you're hiding it.

Physical copies are still the best all of these years later, whenever I receive a shipment of my own paperback novels, it always puts a smile on my face, although I no longer cry tears of joy like I did that first time. That first-time feeling only happens once.

Creating content for social media, especially videos has always been hard for me to do because when I first started I tended to get shy and tongue tied, but whenever I do a video it always receives a higher engagement. At first, I have been recording more of them to get used to it talking on camera. I don't always have a new book to talk about for the videos, so what I have done instead is talk about things I think my characters would like and lately for me its been all about food. I have been posting how to cooking videos on my characters favorite dishes. It is an extra source of engagement and the bonus is I am able to complete them in less takes. I have also started playing around with the silly filters that some of the social media sites have and I find doing videos on the trending filters takes any sort of nerves I had about being on camera and tosses those feelings away and they are always fun. I just put social media and fun together, what?! Some of those filters are hilarious and it's easy content because you don't have to think about a thing its all about how you react to it. Those trends with popular filters tend to give a bunch of unique views so they are not only fun but they give you visibility.

For the text to speech now, for me, its now built in to Microsoft Word. This just goes to show how quickly technology changes.

The way I work today hasn't changed all that much, its been more fine tuning the process that Im used to doing allowing me to do a bit each day but not being so hard on myself that I can't enjoy my time with family. Like way back when I started out writing I still always have some projects on the go at different stages of progress. I do this because if I am having a bit of writers block for a story, I am working on I can switch gears and work on another project that is in the editing stage. This works for me and its just easy for me to keep a flow going rather then get stumped on something and think about it while doing nothing. With multiple projects you can pause one and pick up on another and I find this gives my brain a break for the things I'm stuck on.

I do still enter into writing competitions when I can but have opted to enter those that are free instead of having to pay an entry fee. I no longer send my works to "Library & Archives Canada" It was never a mandatory action and it was resources spent on something that hasn't benefited me in the past. I never received any publicity or recognition for it so I stopped sending them copies of my works. I find now I do a lot of reflection of the tasks that I do in asking myself things like, "How does doing this help me?", "Do I have to do this?" or "What will happen if I don't do this?" When you start to be honest in your response you realize the time, effort and resources you can hold onto and put towards something else and for me I have personally focused more time, effort and resources towards marketing and that's your takeaway for this chapter.

Chapter 9
Nine Months In – Using Coupons to Promote

Then…

It is hard to believe that another month is already over. So, the update for this month is I have now submitted, "A Life Cycle Reborn" to Writers Digest and the Amazon CreateSpace competition and feel great that I didn't shy away and submitted. I also tried something new for the first time. When you self-publish to Smashwords and Amazon both sites have tools in place to adjust the pricing to whatever you wish. For me I have kept my e-book around the $5 mark, (it's a little different from country to country because of exchange rates) So for the first time I used the coupon manager that Smashwords offers and marked my book 50% off for the week that Smashwords was promoting a site sale. As I look back on my sales and the number of downloads, I have to ask myself, did the discount help? To answer that, it's a yes and a no. I did receive a bit of a spike in sample downloads but what I found was that the coupons weren't actually used. So, the no, is I didn't see an increase in sales.

The next question I need to ask myself, is will I participate in future sales promotions and to answer that, I think I will refrain for now and my reasoning is this, during the time that Smashwords was promoting the sales week, I did my own personal promotion with scheduling an extra four tweets a day on twitter and also sending out messages over Facebook directing followers to the site and providing the coupon code. I think that the increase that I saw with sample downloads was from my own personal effort. I would never say that I would never participate in another sale, I just think with this experience is that people purchase books that intrigue them and not because a book is on sale. For me, if I am looking at a book and want to read more, I never say, "Shucks, that is the regular price; I will wait for a sale." For me if I want to read it, I purchase it without a care on if I am getting it at a discount or not and I think that I am not alone in that way of thinking.

My book has been on the market for nine months now and each month I make the effort to branch out and try different things to help my book reach readers and with having the opportunity of participating in a site sale has given me the opportunity to see what it actually is, how it works and how it impacts your book. I am happy that I did it and gained some valuable insight.

Now...

In re-reading this chapter its easy to say that I have tested out a lot of things and for this chapter, for me the competitions, site sales and coupons haven't given me the results that I had hoped for in generating and equal return of sales. I have narrowed my submissions to competitions only applying to free ones. The ones that have an entry fee I feel are not really worth it. They do provide you with feedback so at least you are getting something as opposed to nothing with paying for an entry fee but the thing is feedback can be free. Your readers write reviews, which is a kind of feedback. Did they like the book? Yes or no, why didn't they like it or why did they like it? They will usually share a sentence or two. That's the thing with being an indie author is you have to watch out for your hard-earned money and try to place your bets on things that will generate a positive return. There seems to be a business around making indie authors pay for things that should be free, like reviewers, I have had people tell me that they loved my book and for the small payment of (insert cost) they will post a kind review of my book... Or enter my book competition for (insert cost) and we will decide who wins, in about a year from now, or even pay me (insert cost) and I will have my tweet team promote your book. I have participated in the competitions but everything else I declined. Lesson learned. I see competitions as a vanity thing, for fun, friendly competition and maybe gain some feedback but these competitions don't garner enough exposure to generate sales.

About the coupons, I use them regularly but not just for the site promotions. Site promotions gain a few extra downloads if I'm giving away free copies but rarely do, I gain any extra money. The people browsing for deals on the site promotions only seem to be looking for free books and this is my own personal experience. What I have done over the years is use coupons for different purposes like providing them to my Facebook and twitter followers, the people that have supported me over the years, whenever I produce a new title, I will post the free coupon codes for them to download my latest novels for a limited time. I do this as a thank you and it also creates a better opportunity of them reading my novel and providing a review or promoting it to their own connections.

For the price point I try to set the price aligning myself with the prices of books that are similar to mine and even all of these years later my views on price haven't changed. I think books fall into a category where if it is on sale or not won't be the deciding factor in whether or not a reader buys a book. I think if your price aligns with the market, whether its on sale doesn't really matter, through there is one exception. If you have a series or many books and you are still relatively unknown then I think discounting your first book in the series or one of your books can help because the reader has not much to lose with a tiny purchase and if they enjoyed your discounted book chances are that they will return and buy your other books at the regular price.

In Short...

Competitions are great if they are free. They challenge you, it gets your work out there and even if you don't win its experience. Proceed with caution on paid competitions, for the cost of the entry fee, what you get out of it if you don't win is minimal. For the one I entered I received a review of my work and that was it.

Coupons can be a good thing and you can get creative in using them. They are not just for site wide promotions. I have used them to give as gifts to followers.

For price point stay close to the medium and don't feel obligated to discount all your books just because. If you have several books I suggest discounting one to attract new readers but in short don't sell yourself short. This is your writing and hard work and you deserve to be valued fairly.

Chapter 10
Ten & Eleven Months In – Finding a Routine, Social
Media, Writing a Trilogy

Then…

It is not long before I mark off a year of having self-published my first book. I am comfortable with the routine that I have created. I send out tweets daily, with the help of a program called Hootsuite. It allows me to time posts and also helps me free up my schedule. I also send Facebook posts daily, which has become easy for me to do. I used to struggle with this because Facebook has very interactive users, so coming up with something unique was hard at times. I know that some of my posts have been absolute flops because of the built-in analytics feature. With analytics, I have learned that the more personal messages are the ones do the best. So, my advice is to pay attention to how much engagement your posts receive and adjust accordingly to your audience while continuing to be your authentic self.

Another part of my daily routine is to work on my own writing and read other books, and after dinner is the best time for me. While my husband watches Criminal Minds, CSI, and Bates Motel, I often have my iPhone out, putting words to my note pad application to write my books. Today, I have two more books written and I am approaching 20,000 words into my third book. My plan for this trilogy is to have it all written and edited first, and then I will publish the books one at a time and space out the release dates by 6 months to 1 year.

My reasoning for spacing them out is to give the books a bit of time to gain a following and allow them to stand out on their own. I admit I am still in the toddler stage of having a grasp on the business side of selling books, but what I have absorbed in the time that I have spent at the craft is this, I have sat back and watched others take this approach and the successful authors who have trilogies seem to allow a bit of a grace period between books and if the formula works for them, it should do the same for me.

I make the effort to read other authors books daily and I find the time to do this before going to sleep. I love reading a story to relax. It helps me get my mind off of the things in my daily life and for a moment in time, I forget about my worries and get absorbed into the story. The other reason why I read is to keep my mind fresh, absorb the style of the author in their writing and learn new writing techniques.

Other things that I have had happened to me in the past couple of months, is people that I have had the privilege of being able to talk to on social media have opened up with their own experiences. I had talked about this in my post titled, "Three Months In" and I can't explain enough how eye opening it is to get to learn about the lives that others from around the world. People are truly amazing and they may or may not know but they are helping me to better understand the world and maybe the insights into their lives will help strengthen my own story telling.

So, what's next for me? I had a goal of publishing my next book on the anniversary release date of my first published book, "A Life Cycle Reborn" (June 3rd) but as it is now, I am not ready because I am deep into the editing phase and have only just begun with having test readers provide their feedback on the story. Being a self-published author, I have the choice to choose when to release my new book and for now, I want to put more work into it before publishing.

Moving forward, I am continuing to put the effort into writing my third book to the trilogy and editing the first two books, my goal is to stay focused and come up with a polished, top notch trilogy.

Now…

Oh boy, all I can say is all that work I talked about back then with posting everyday and using applications to help automate it was indeed still a lot of work. I no longer use applications to automate posts even with the automation it was still a lot and not to mention you start to lose that feeling of being your authentic self because it is work coming up with content and then being social with it in replying to the comments. I may go back to it some day but for now its hard to manage writing, coming up with content daily and being a mom (since 2018). I have scaled back on posting social media content and instead post weekly. I have expanded the social media sites that I'm on so I have expanded in that sense and depending on the medium I'll sometimes reuse content like sharing a picture on Twitter, Instagram and Facebook while posting a video to TicTok and YouTube. Once a week works for me right now where I can focus on work & family. I try to interact daily with others in my social media networks. I give myself twenty minutes in the morning while having a coffee to browse the feeds and see what everyone is up to and engage in others content, though its more like every other day, just because twenty minutes isn't always enough time to view all the social media sites! I would like to be more engaging, this schedule works best for me at the moment and that's okay. Some Author's post several times a day while other best-selling author's have no online presence at all and wherever you fall on the spectrum is okay. The best thing is to do what you are comfortable with and if you want to take on more or less than do it. I have learned that it really doesn't matter. Your connections won't forget about you, they may not even realize you have taken some time away.

The other thing I talked about was spacing out my novels and boy have I done that. It took years to publish, "A Life Again", the sequel to, "A Life Cycle Reborn" it wasn't by choice, it was because a few things had happened while working on it. I had a writer's block and then once I started back up at working on it I had forgotten where I had left off and had to re-read it and on top of that I was writing from multiple characters points of view so I had to figure out the timeline and proper order of the chapters. This really slowed my progress however I was able to eventually finish and publish the book. I learned that I will never just write a story without having a plot of the chapters drafted first. So now what I do is I write summaries of how I want a chapter to go and when I am ready to write the chapter in full, I have a summary to look at as a writing prompt. My next books I hope to not go beyond a year in between books. Reading is still one of my favorite past times. I just love falling into a great story and as always I read as a way to unwind before bed, unless I'm on vacation, then you may find me lazing at the beach with a book in hand. I still read other authors books and I try to write and post reviews for the books that I enjoyed. I look at it as an opportunity to engage with others, both readers and authors. I use Goodreads, Wattpad and Medium.

Going back to engagement, I can't say that I have as many one on one conversations with others online as I did when I first started and that is partly on me. Time is so limited for everyone and though I have the occasional one on one discussion with others online, carving out time doesn't always fit in with life and like I mentioned before it is on me because I made the choice to step back from social media to focus more on family, the work and balancing life without having to follow a rigid routine and this has helped in so many ways.

Though my family has grown I have found more time to write, improve my skills and just give myself time to breathe and think out my next steps with the various writing projects that are underway. "A Life Freed" will be my next Earth & Airus Series novel.

Chapter 11
One Year In – The End of being a Newbie

Then…

Here I am writing, this just a few days before my anniversary of having published, "A Life Cycle Reborn", my sci-fi, fantasy, time-travel novel and I can say that as I look back on this year brings a smile to my face. It has been eye-opening. I have learned that if you want to achieve something you can, there is nothing holding you back.

Some of the things that I had assumed are for sure not the case, at least not yet. Like, I am not a famous Author and I still can't quit my day job, BUT I have not given up on that dream. I know that with writing books, publishing and promoting your work takes a lot of guts, work, effort and an open mind. I will continue to work at it because I count my achievements in my writing career as steps toward this goal.

I will focus on social media to promote and I realize now, that it is a constantly changing environment and that you have to learn to adjust. Earlier in this book, I had mentioned reach with Facebook and a year ago, when I had provided the numbers was before Facebook had changed their algorithms and now when I post information to my page, my reach has gone from hundreds of thousands to just hundreds. The reason for that is I understand that they want us to pay for reach and it's a way for Facebook to generate revenue. I will keep the page up but I will also consider other social media channels because I am not at a point in my career where I can afford to pay for marketing; not yet!

Also, in previous chapters, I had talked about targeting the right audience for my book. The funny thing now, is when I read that chapter, I realize that back then, I had absolutely no clue who my target audience was and now after a year of sales and gaining fans, I had been completely wrong.

I wrote an Adventure, Sci-fi, Fantasy novel, but the feel of it is Young Adult. I thought because it was written with a first person, young adult flavor that my audience would be exactly that, young adult. The truth is more men (aged 35-45) have purchased my book. My fans are primarily men and they count for about 70% of my fan base.

I have to take a step back and ask what genre is this book and the answer is science fiction. The book is about time travel, following the life of a woman who lived a life on Earth but recalls in a previous life that she lived on another planet. There is some romance, some adventure and some young adult content, but the main focus is science fiction and that genre has a huge male following. It took a year to learn this because it takes time to sell books and build a fan base and now, I will take this new-found information and move forward.

On a career level, I am not a famous author yet so I still have a day job. I just had my performance review with my boss last week and moving forward she is going to continue to have me focus on learning the art of marketing. I had attended some social media courses this past year but have not yet had the chance to job shadow and she is recommending to her boss that I do this task to help her as well as help me with my skills. I am a believer in constant learning and after a year, I know that I need more effort put towards marketing.

So this marks a year of learning how to swim in the Author world, and I encourage anyone wanting to take this route, do it because you want to, keep an open mind, make sure to stay current with writing topics, stay up to date on articles, I use google frequently. Get on social media and start being social. Make connections with other creative people and as you put an effort towards promotion, a fan base will follow. Read books to keep your brain fresh and sharp and find a routine.

Now...

Most of the above still holds true, and in continuing to write and publish more books the opportunity is there to gain more readers. It can take years to become a well-known author because you are building your content, adjusting to the trends and establishing your brand. I suggest to keep writing and publishing if it is something that brings you joy. I know for myself, with every book that I publish, it brings me happiness with it being a creative outlet, it brings me a sense of achievement and every published product creates the opportunity to attract more readers.

When and opportunity presents it self try to take it. If you have funds for promoting on social media advertisements, try it out. When a distributer is running a site wide promotion, opt your books into the promotion. If you have an opportunity to socialize offline like in an author event participate. I still have not done it in person, I will eventually but I can say that last fall I participated in Wattpad's Writers Connect event in which I was able to network online with fellow writers. It was so much fun.

Try other things besides social media to promote. Like this year I have been getting more focused on Amazon paid ads and trying out the different kinds of promotional tools they have, giving the ad campaigns time to build analytics and then adjusting the campaigns to try to improve the results. You can run multiple ads at once and you can go in at anytime and edit the campaign.

The thing is even after years of being an active author there is still so much to learn and try especially when it comes to marketing your work and all you need to do is try in order to see if whatever it is works for you. You need to be aware that the rules are constantly changing. What works on Facebook today may not work tomorrow. Also, distributors come and go so try to not put your eggs all in one basket and be aware of all your options should a distributer close their business. I have seen two sunsets with CreateSpace and Pronoun and just recently Smashwords has been purchased by Draft2Digital. Things are constantly changing so keep on top of the news by following your distributors, so that you can make things work to your advantage.

This right here would have been the end of this book and it was at one point but with reopening this book and working on a major edit to reflect on the "Then" versus "Now" there is still more to talk about and so we have arrived to the next part.

The Next Part

These next chapters are laid out differently because it's additional content. In the introduction to this book I explained that how the chapters followed a then and now format because the original chapters were reflections of my experiences as a new author in 2013 and the now was my current reflections.

These next chapters are added thoughts and lessons learned based on my own experiences that concern different things and topics, so onto the next part!

Chapter 12
Social Media Sites

I am being upfront. I have a love hate relationship with social media. I love reading up about others, seeing what friends are up to and seeing what's going on in general. I have been on Facebook and Twitter since I first started publishing novels but being social for me isn't easy. I am an introvert and I don't know what to say or post most of the time. Before publishing my first book, I read many self-publishing books that explained the importance of using social media to market your author brand. I had also attended a few seminars on the topic. It isn't a new concept but for an introvert it is easier said than done.

The common messages were, post regularly, balance marketing posts and personal posts so that your followers stay engaged and be yourself. I try to follow this and in the beginning it felt awkward. I am shy by nature so racking my brain on what to post was the effort. I started off in following a daily schedule with posting things to all of my social media platforms, I used a tool called HuiteSuite to automate some of the posts. The forcing myself to post regularly helped me overcome the bulk of the shyness and it also gave me material that I could review in being able to measure my analytics. I found insight and for me that cookie cutter approach was a starting point but it wasn't the best approach as I learned after reviewing engagement levels. I'll explain my stats later the point that I am getting to is I had Facebook, Twitter and Google+ and now the next site to be on was

Goodreads. I was like why, because don't the other social media sites cover it all and don't these platforms combined have millions of users? What is the point in using Goodreads?

Goodreads has been around for a while but I admit that it☐is a newer endeavor for me. I have had a Goodreads account for a couple of years but between writing and editing books and marketing myself on the major social media platforms (Facebook, Twitter and Google+) Goodreads had taken a back seat with getting my attention.

After only using Facebook, Twitter and Google+ and promoting my first published novel for just over a year on the other social media sites I decided to give Goodreads more attention. My reasons were because I was used to the tasks and I was finding that my book sales were predictable and I wanted to try something different as a way to increase my reach and boost sales. I made time for Goodreads by scaling back on the other social media sites.

I used to post something daily but changed the routine to posting once or twice a week. The thing with Facebook is my followers don't really care for the business side of things, like book promoting and such, they are more interested on what is happening in my life. They engage in posts that give insight on what I am up to or like or things that I am working on. They engage that way. so, if I post something about a novel I am working on, I'll receive engagement versus if I post information on where my books are for sale, I'll get little to no engagement. I think the reasons are two-fold because people know where to buy books, and they already know that I have books for sale from my link in bio, so posting about books for sale is redundant.

The routine I described earlier helped me get comfortable with being open and I am more willing to share but the other side of it is, if your Facebook fans are not actively interacting on your page with liking posts or commenting, your page will eventually stop showing on their newsfeed and that is even if they liked your page. It's a constant battle for views and engagement and I hate that part of it, in knowing that the applications are constantly changing visibility pf posts, and over the years I have lightened my schedule and adopted a once a week routine because for me, putting the effort forward to come up with new content daily, knowing that post visibility is in question, its not worth the effort, if only a handful of people see it.

I have scaled back with Twitter too. I still post a few posts a week and I have Hootsuite helping me with posting promotional tweets but the thing with Twitter is it is a noisy place. Everyone is tweeting and trying to be heard and it's the opposite of Facebook, your followers will see your tweets on the newsfeed but if they are following thousands of others your posts become lost in the noise.

I decided to focus more on Goodreads because I had read a few author blogs saying that Goodreads was the best tool for authors since a coffee machine. I know I'm like a sheep. The thing was that I kept seeing mentions like that over and over again and at first I didn't get it. I didn't understand because as a reader on Goodreads I can see that I can network with friends and add books to the bookshelves on my profile, rate books and once you reached a certain number of reviews Goodreads will start to recommend books to you. That's great for the avid reader and that's how I personally used Goodreads.

Now as an author there is more, you can tag the books that you have written on your profile, market yourself with running promotions such as book giveaways, participate as a reader or author. Goodreads is the place where you can find your niche market. If you write sci-fi you can focus efforts on sci-fi readers, if you write romance, fantasy whatever, you can target those readers in your marketing efforts. Goodreads makes this so easy that they have categorized genres for authors to promote. The nice thing is when readers take notice they can become a fan this is shared with their own network of friends.

Also, let's say that you do a give away on Goodreads, you kind of get a two for one promotion deal. One is the initial book give away promotional add. When the winners are determined and the books are mailed to the winners the second promotion is that those readers may rate your book and provide a review. There is a third thing too, in that your book giveaway garnered thousands of views and interest and even though those people didn't win a copy of your book you have assurance that they know your book exists and they may be motivated to purchase their own copy. It's not a requirement of the winners to write reviews but these readers for one thing are more motivated to do so than your average reader since they are on a book review site and they just won a free book. If you get a review from the winners, I would consider that your fourth promotion as their review will reach their network of friends.

Before I end this chapter I stress that even though the other social media sites aren't really geared for promoting books don't delete your accounts. Even though the goal is to not spread yourself thin, the goal is also not to put all of your eggs in one basket. This chapter was written when Google+ had a social media site and now it doesn't. Anyways, going back to Goodreads a d having other social media sites you still you can make these social media sites work together and with Goodreads you can find other Goodreads users through your other social media accounts. There is a "find friends" setting and Goodreads will send out friend invites to your other social media circles like Twitter and Facebook. I may sound lazy with taking a bit of a step back from the major social media sites but let's face it, a writer's goal is to focus their time in writing books and making the effort to get their book out there. Social media can be a time hog and if you are starting out and doing it all on your own I recommend Goodreads to try. It has strong marketing tools and the focus is readers and books.

Chapter 13
Being yourself

Be yourself! That's the end of this chapter! Just kidding! I can't stress it enough. If you are not yourself people pick up on it, they get board of you and will eventually ignore your social media content.

I have read many times of those giving advice on how to layer your posts and it completely makes sense to me. Layering means balancing your content. If you do want to regularly talk about your books you need to not do it for every single post and I have read and tried to follow as best as I can using the rule of thirds. Post about things happening in your life besides promoting your books. Share what you are comfortable sharing and be yourself. Talk about things you love. You are a writer, share articles on some of your own favorite writers. You are sharing with your audience the things that you love, you are showing confidence in your own skills by not being afraid to mention other writers and you are doing good by promoting others. Lastly mention your own work and I really mean promote yourself at most a third of the time because let's face it people get tired of seeing the same things over again and social media is about being social, it's not called promotional media! I would even say do it far less than a third of the time. Instead mention your books and provide links to your books in your biography. When someone follows you, try to introduce yourself and be friendly or have some sort of welcome message pinned to the top of your page.

I know that in the beginning I was really nervous about opening up online and in a pubic platform but I pushed on and posted things that I was comfortable in sharing. As a follower of other authors, I notice that some share everything from what they eat, to where they are and when they are on vacation while others maintain very private profiles though they manage to still post content. One author I follow never posts any pictures or videos of herself and what she does is she does a lot of chapter reads as though she is doing a mini podcast and for a visual, she displays her branding while she reads or talks about what she is working on.

Being yourself and being comfortable with what you say or do online in a public setting matters and you need to be comfortable with what to share and also you need to be comfortable with the schedule you choose to post. My recommendation is to pick a frequency and try to stay with it as best as you can and if you need to adjust then do so because your audience is waiting for you and you should maintain a level of frequency that works for you.

Chapter 14
Popularity Contest

This topic is similar to the chapter on being yourself. I think that you need to be yourself always to reach a level of popularity but there is more to it and popularity is more than being yourself. I have not fully grasped this topic but these are the observations that I have made.

There is a chapter in this book title Wattpad, which is a social media site where authors publish their works for free and there is a huge reader base that votes and comments on the stories. This fuels buzz and authors either become popular on this site or they don't.

The reader base from what I can see is that a huge chunk of its users ranges from being in their teens and twenties.

I have participated as both an author and as a reader. As a reader I have read some of the works of others, popular and not so popular and great books have a lot of followers, they are popular and it makes sense. Great books deserve popularity. I also found that there are also two types of authors that have these popular books, ones that are active on the Wattpad community and ones who are not. So in theory if you have a great book that book should do well and get votes and gain a follower base. Sounds too easy right?

On the flip side there are also those who have books that have gained votes and a follower base and I have read them. To be honest the books didn't do it for me. They were full of errors, holes in the story and chapters would just drag on. So why or how do these books become so popular on Wattpad? The answer to this is that from what I see the authors of these books are very active on the site, they communicate with other users, participate in Wattpad's community, they have become liked and my feeling is that the friends that they have made have supported their work by providing them with votes and the friends have been forgiving of the level of writing that has been produced. Another thing with these popular stories is that the author has written about things that already have a huge fan base. So, for example they have chosen a popular boy band and created a story around an established group.

Popularity has no set formula and it is an interesting concept because it can happen in many ways. If you have a great book it should succeed, it takes a couple of readers to read it, vote for it and follow the author and once people start to read it seems to move up in visibility on the rankings lists. I see some popular authors engage like crazy while other popular authors barely touch their social media feeds. If your book isn't so great you can still make it popular thru being active on the site and if you play nice as in be polite, read other peoples work, provide comments to the feeds and give back in that sense, popularity will follow with people engaging with you, following you and eventually checking out your own stories.

Spending time on these sites, not just Wattpad is something to consider if you are trying to grow your audience and your books visibility and again that's the love/hate relationship that I have with social media. What do you want? What time can you afford to it? What is your comfort level with socializing? See how these basic themes keep coming to light!

Chapter 15
Promoting

There is so many tips and resources on this topic and you have to ask yourself first, how much time are you willing to commit? What platforms are you going to use? I am always making the effort to try different things, some work and some don't and that's okay because it is something that you need to figure out.

Switching lanes for a moment. I love watching reality TV and right now I'm into the show, "Alone", which takes ten hard core survivalists and it puts them into the wilderness alone, they are separated by five miles and they are to survive on their own for as long as it takes until they are the last person standing. The winner gets half a million. Anyway, every single participant is and expert outdoors person, they all have strong skills and no one person is more skilled then their competitor. They are all allowed to bring ten items of their choosing, like hunting gear, tools, camping gear, clothing and they use those items to help them survive. Immediately you see how even if different participants are fishing as a way to feed themselves, they have the same fishing lines and same hooks and they are fishing in the same bodies if water, but some catch a ton of fish while others nothing, they are fishing the same way, trying a variety of techniques but some just don't get a bite and ultimately have to make the choice, keep fishing or try to hunt for other food.

One thing, even if you follow step by step a method to promoting it may work for one person but not another. Promoting yourself is trying to find something that works for you and learning when to move on when its not working. I'll provide you here all the things that I have done and share what worked and what didn't.

Social media works, it's free, your reach is good but for me I find that I need to be aware of my time spent online and that I need to post a majority of content that is social and not only post about promoting my books. My followers start to lose interest if all my content involves just talking about my books. This ties in to being yourself. If people like you they will check your biographies and in them, include the links to all the sites where your work is for sale. See how all of these chapters relate?

Ensure that whatever platforms that you have put your work on that your profile information is kept up to date, so for me the sites that I use are Amazon KDP, Smashwords and Draft2Digital and those three sites combined distribute to other vendors and worldwide that the content on those sites are kept up to date.

Other methods to help promote is I have read that starting a blog is a great tool to help promote yourself and your work. I started my own, I don't make time to keep up on it. I'm on the fence with it because I question, do celebrities keep webpages or have they pivoted to using the social media sites as their stages? Do people visit websites? I put time into building it, I see potential, and have not given up on the site. Aside from promoting yourself remember do what makes you happy and that applies to promotion also. Even though my blog hasn't given me much of a return yet in terms of promotion, I enjoy having a spot that's my own on the Internet and journaling what is happening, my work, and I am using the blog as a place to tie all of my social media and my online footprint together.

What I mean by this is with sites such as Facebook, Twitter, Goodreads, Pinterest and Wattpad you can use widgets from those social media sites and put them on your blog to tie everything together. Widgets are great because it shows your blog visitors where you are active. If you aren't an active blogger these widgets produce activity on you blog. Like for example I am active on Twitter and though I may not be an active blogger the Twitter widget shows my visitors the latest activity from me.

Other avenues to take is giving away free books. You can do this without spending money. I have done this with eBooks and you have a few helpful resources at your finger tips. On Smashwords, and KDP you can simply post your eBook as free. You are the creator of your work and the master of what goes and you can decide how long you want your content made free. All you do is re-list the book as free. People love free. Once it's free, post the news on your social media sites, your blog. People tend to be more open to giving a book a chance if it's of no cost to them because there isn't risk. Without asking for it, some will even grace you with a review and that's music to an indie authors ear. A review good or bad has a secondary affect of promoting. It means that you are no longer alone in promoting as the reviews that are posted about your books are shared with that reviewers' social circles, which means that they are reaching people that you may have never been able to reach. I personally have only used the Smashwords feature with their site wide sales and using their coupon generator to mark books down for free. For me I received downloads, I received some reviews, but ultimately, I think that you marking books down to free is not something that you would want to do often. I think like anything that the excitement wears off if you often mark things for free and I think if you fall down that hole your followers may come to expect free. I'm not against free, my thought is if you are going to post for free then to do it sparingly.

I have tried using coupons and for me coupons had no effect on selling more books. I think the reasoning behind it is that the titles that I currently have are under $5.00, they are of little cost as it is so perhaps if my books were at the $10.00 mark I may have gotten more results in discounting my work but for me I didn't get a positive from it.

Pivoting while keeping on the topic of free is that for my most recent novel, "The Crinkled Page" before I published it. I offered advanced reader copies to my social media followers to garner interest and generate reviews and I found that beneficial because it did a few things. It did generate social media content, it did reward my followers, it did provide me with reviews and it did expand my reach from my followers re-sharing posts and their reviews would have reached their own social circles that I wouldn't have been able to reach.

Promoting is such a huge area and I realize that I have only touched on things geared to online and my personal experiences with promoting is just a fraction of suggestions, though be reminded that these are my own attempts and the experiences that came with doing them.

Chapter 16
Fans the good and the bad

Even if you are not a famous author, publishing your work and putting yourself out their publicly will draw attention, your work will eventually be read and you will gain fans. There is literally billions of us, so even if your book isn't for mainstream it should land with others.

For me I sort of knew through hearing interviews by celebrities that they will get a fan who is passionate about them, wanting more than what a typical fan would want and that is attention from the celebrity. For myself I have always trusted my gut, be open when you are comfortable in doing so and when something doesn't feel right don't participate, remove your self from the situation.

Do you know what a troll is? Most do but in case that you don't, they are people that deliberately provoke others online. They feed off of the hurt that they cause and the attention that they receive in doing so. Trolls will make their ugly appearance, posting a negative and hurtful comment about you or your work and my advice is don't respond. I never have though I admit that when I got my first troll encounter I can't say that reading their comments didn't hurt. They did big time hurt but you know what most platforms give you the ability to report the comments and request to the site to remove them and most sites from my own personal experience oblige.

Its okay for readers to not like your book but a negative review is one thing and a personal attack is another and if something doesn't sit well with you, say something. Personally, I don't get the motivation behind causing hurt to others I really don't and now that I'm older I just don't bother to let it eat away at me like I did when I started, I don't have the time or energy to sink to their level and hand it back to them.

Trolls were the bad for me. I remember getting stomach aches after reading their hurtful comments. The other bad is the opposite of a troll, someone who likes your writing so much that they plagiarize it. Thankfully I have never had to deal with a plagiarist though it happens. I recommend keeping proof of your copyright. In Canada you can register your work with the federal government's copyright office and receive a copyright certificate. You can also go as far as email yourself a copy of your work so that it is time stamped and you can also go as far as saving your work to a thumb drive putting it in an envelope and mailing it to yourself and not opening the envelope so that you have proof that you are the creator and you have the original copy.

I have heard that if you have an instance of someone plagiarising your work and it is up on a distributer site you can contact both the distributor and the plagiarist to having the work removed.

To avoid plagiarism of my work, I have chosen to publish my work on as many sites as I can rather than just publishing to one site. Yes, wide distribution allows you to tap into a variety of customers but the other side of it is that it is also security in making sure your work isn't published by someone else.

Most fans are fantastic, funny, clever and nice. Most will be your champions in helping to create awareness of your work. Most are respectful online. Most are people who have chosen to follow you for a variety of reasons and your job is again to be yourself, engage and write!

Chapter 17
Blog sites

This is new for me and I have no idea if this is going to be a fit. Currently I have started a blog, and have a few posts on it along with widgets to my other social media sites. Having my own blog isn't really a fit for me. I have it, its still live but I am not doing much with it. The only thing that stays up to date is the social media carousels.

Should I keep it up? I don't know, probably no but then again, its hard to rationalize deleting the work that you have already put into it. For now, I am going to leave it alone and just focus on the sites that people are visiting and there is nothing wrong with that in fact I could visit other people's blogs and go on a blog tour with my books. A blog tour is when you pay someone to organize a feature and they turn around and promote your feature to bloggers who then choose to pick it up to promote on their own blogs. It's a great set up and I have done this before and it generates sales and even reviews. If you can afford it and you can dedicate a little more time to helping the organizer create content. They will send you a list of items they are looking for you to provide. Usually an image of your cover, author photo, a book blurb, a sampling of chapters, links on where to purchase and sometimes interview questions.

If your someone who has a blog and its current it may be of interest to feature other authors or join forces with other authors in order to create content. There are sites that are focused around this concept though I can't say if its labour intensive, or if it generates sales because I have never tried it, though it is something on my radar to look into more. The reason why I haven't tried is because my blog has been asleep for years and I feel like I would need to breathe more life into it first before teaming up with other's.

Going off on a side thought for a moment. Though I have not really embraced my own blog I feel like all of the social media sites are kind of like mini blogs of their own. Depending on the platform, you are sharing, photos, an update, or videos. Across all of the social media platforms that's enough to create content for a blog, so why not blog it?

I only need to convince myself and try again or leave it be and its your choice to. Do you create a space that's your own and use it as a tool to join marketing forces with other authors?

I'll leave it at that for this chapter.

Chapter 18
Pen name

Why not right? If you are an author like me that dabbles in different genres, using a pen names helps identify that separation of your work.

I mainly write in fantasy and science fiction and keep those books listed under my name and I also write romance, which I opted for a pen name. I have this book under "how to" and a children's book underway which I think I'll keep under my own name just because they are smaller projects and the readers I don't think will have and expectation that the how too is a science fiction or fantasy novel. For the children's book, I wanted to do something special for my son and so for his next birthday I wrote him a story about what his favorite teddy bear does while he is away during the day. I felt that keeping it under my name made sense as I don't think I'll be writing a lot of children's books, so I don't think there is a need for a pen name to separate genres. This one was more of a labor of love project.

I consider pen names as a way to organize your work. Some authors also do it for fun or even for the challenge. I know of one author that published in fantasy and had great success and she decided that she wanted to write in crime fiction but didn't want her well known name help promote sales in this new genre for her. She wanted a challenge, to see if she could succeed a second time but in the crime fiction genre. She wrote under a male pen name and ended up reaching fame a second time with her pen name.

The only downfall with using pen names is because the names keep your works separate it means that you have to start from scratch with building your fan base for each name, though if you look on the upside of it, each name you use to define each kind of book you put out is like casting multiple lines out in the water and the more lines you cast the better the odds of finding a great reader base that connects with a specific style of your writing.

Chapter 19
Spreading yourself thin

Use these platforms. Read these advice sites. Join my mailing list. Write, edit, read. Participate in blogs. Join a readers group. Enter these writing competitions. Be present on social media sites. If you allow it, you will see tons of suggestions, recommendations, advice on what you need to do, what you should do and how often you need do it and I even have a say on it. You have picked up this book and you are reading of my own experiences and opinions to all of these topics. Whether you do all of them, a couple of them or none is completely up to you. My advice is do what you can while still maintaining a life outside of writing. All of these tasks and suggestions can be done by one author but doing it all and not allowing yourself a manageable time frame is stretching yourself thin.

Writing can take you down many paths and this hobby has the potential to become a full time job with a team of support helping you out and it's how far you decide that you want to take it and it is relatively easy to take this hobby and turn it into a business because self publishing has so many easy to use online tools that help you publish a variety of content and you also have an array of marketing tools at your fingertips as well as distributors and you can do it all in the comfort of your home.

I have been working at my writing for years and although I don't have enough time to do everything that I want to in a day I keep it in my mind to that the things that you can accomplish will matter tomorrow, next week, next month and next year. Do what you can do today and try to make it the best that you can. As I write these words I am writing them in the moments of free time that I have and I am doing it on my phone to transfer to a document later on. I likely won't complete this chapter today and admit that I didn't even start this chapter today, but this time matters, these moments I have are of value and they are adding up and eventually this book will be complete. I don't have an hour of free time to create the perfect writing situation of having a cup of coffee, my laptop opened and ready in a quiet office with zero interruption. That's not happening here and if I tried to create that environment I would need to wait at least a week because I am not even at home right now.

I am not putting pressure on myself to spread my time thin and instead I give myself the opportunity in having my phone at my fingertips because when a thought or something pops into my head then I have the opportunity to add those thoughts to my notes and its easy, relaxing and no stress. I feel great that I could capture a couple of sentences of thoughts and as life pulls me away from my writing. That is okay because I can pick up where I left off in the next moment of calm.

If you have no interest in working the way that I do, that's okay but realizing that you can't do it all and discovering the life hacks to do what you can then do it.

I save my work frequently. I pay for services where I know I need the help and stay within my budget and I adjust my timelines to make sure that for the things I want to do myself eventually get done.

You will know if you spread yourself thin if these to do things feel like work, are no longer fun and the content your creating doesn't have that special something that makes you smile. When you fall into this space, stop, step back, and reflect on what you can do to simplify tasks and make them easy fun and fair to yourself so that you can achieve them without breaking your spirit.

Chapter 20
Wattpad

This application provides a platform where writers can write, save drafts and publish one chapter at a time until their work is complete. The site provides writers an audience of readers who can engage in the writing and each other.

The site also provides a variety of writing contests, writing opportunities as well as publishing opportunities.

If you are new to the idea of wanting to share your writing with others, this application is a great place to share your work or keep your writing private until you are ready. If your story has reached fame it's still a great place to reach more readers and if you are somewhere in between, the site has what you need to dip your toes into practicing your craft, engaging with others, participating in events, competitions and calls for submissions.

I recommend this site to try and practice ideas and as you get comfortable with the many aspects of being an author you can take your lessons learned from using Wattpad and branch out. Test the foundation that Wattpad has taught you and apply it to other services available to you. Try engaging new readers on other platforms by following similar content, commenting on other posts and providing your own updates. Use hashtags where applicable. Try serialized chapter reveals, and updating your work regularly. Consider cover updates to see what resonates. Change your pitch and blurb to see what attracts more. Test your branding. Use pictures from shoulders up for profile pictures and try to keep the same image throughout all your profiles.

Wattpad has created this unique space for readers and writers and the skills you learn on their site translates to other aspects in your writing work.

I have used Wattpad for years and I find that the site still feels current with the tools and trends that are out now. Wattpad has a team of staff and I find that they often introduce new features, events and when something isn't working they cut it from their site. My only criticisms with the site is sometimes it's hard to get new readers looking at your work unless you are updating or adding chapters often otherwise the visibility tends to slip if you aren't actively writing. My other criticism is that there is more of a younger audience and the trending books tend to be teen, new adult, fan fiction that's based on boy groups. The audience is pivoting and a variety of genres but it seems to be a smaller audience. My last criticism and I am not sure where I stand on this is criticism, is the ability for others to provide their opinions of an author's writing. I'm all for engagement and reviews, it helps and author grow but the thing is it's censored if anyone is offended by a comment it can be removed and reported, which I can completely get and understand because words can hurt and when things go in a negative direction, it doesn't take much to go from, "Meh I didn't like this book." To "This book really sucked and the author should stop writing…"

Writing is hard. Learning that your writing doesn't resonate with readers is even harder. The thing with having these censors is I find everything is positive, I rarely see any comments saying that they didn't like a book or the way a character was represented or anything and I know that there should be a spectrum of positive and negative views so if you are looking for raw feedback, Wattpad isn't the place. You can only see what people are choosing to share with you. As much as it pains me to say this, I commend the site for creating a safe and positive space but as a writer seeking feedback, be aware that you are only receiving part of the picture. A workaround for me in understanding the negative is if a chapter is receiving reads but no comments or likes then there is likely a problem with the chapter that is causing the lack of engagement.

Wattpad is an amazing online tool for writers to use even if they don't know how far they want to go on their personal writing journeys.

Chapter 21
Advertisements

As an author, I used to be a penny-pincher extraordinaire, always on the hunt for cost-free ways to advertise my books. I was so thrifty that I wouldn't spend a dime, thinking that if I wasn't making sales, I shouldn't be spending. However, I've come to realize that it's crucial to invest in yourself, even if you're not turning a profit right away. Everyone has to start somewhere, and if your budget permits, try starting with something small to test the waters and see how your audience responds.

When I look back at my days of not spending on advertising, I realize I learned a lot. I taught myself how to use Adobe Photoshop to create eye-catching posters and crisp images. I learned how to capture videos and photos and use software to create compelling content. By observing and emulating those who excelled on social media, regardless of their niche, I learned how to market myself effectively. I paid attention to what worked and adapted it to my own posts.

I posted my products on a variety of websites, including social media platforms and my own blog, always sticking to free options to stay within my budget. However, I soon realized that organic reach can only get you so far, and most social media sites have built-in paid advertising options. If you're serious about reaching a larger audience, it may be worth considering investing in paid advertising.

I have used paid Facebook ads and let me tell you, it was a mixed bag. At first, I thought it was a great idea, but it turned out to be a mistake. Although Facebook provides tools to narrow down your audience, targeting is not as easy as it seems. I learned this the hard way.

When I tried free advertising, I discovered my target audience: North American men and women aged 25-45 who loved fantasy and science-fiction novels. But when I ran my Facebook advertisements, I struggled to get any sales. First, I posted a picture of a young woman reading my book, which generated some engagement but no sales. Then, I switched to a man in his thirties reading by the river, and I got more engagement from women, but still no sales. Next, I tried a picture of an older man in his fifties reading my book, and while I received a lot of engagement, I still didn't make any sales.

As I changed the pictures, I also tried different messaging and the same call to action to purchase my book, but nothing seemed to work. Eventually, I had to pause the campaign. I realized that I still didn't know who my readers were or how to reach them. Facebook is a huge platform, and my first attempt at running ads didn't yield any return on investment.

But here's the thing: if I ever want to try Facebook ads again, I now know that I need to figure out exactly how to target my audience. It's not enough to have a general idea. So, I'm taking this experience as a learning opportunity and will be more strategic in the future.

If you're selling your books on platforms like Amazon KDP, you have access to analytics that show you where your sales are coming from. In my case, I've been getting most of my sales from Canada, the United States, and Great Britain. Meanwhile, Wattpad provides me with insights into my readership, which is predominantly women between the ages of 18 and 25.

When I first tried advertising my book on Wattpad, I used an image of a young woman reading it, hoping to attract readers who could visualize themselves in that position. Unfortunately, that approach didn't resonate with my target audience. Perhaps it's because Wattpad's user base skews young, and my ad featuring a middle-aged man garnered the most attention on Facebook, which has an average user age of forty.

There are several factors at play here, and it's crucial to take a multi-layered approach to analyzing your data. First, you need to review your analytics to see where your sales are coming from. Then, you must carefully consider which platform you want to advertise on, considering their average user demographics. For instance, if your target audience is young adults, Facebook may not be the best fit for your advertising strategy.

The Facebook ad allows you to advertise on Instagram as well, and I took advantage of this option. Instagram is better suited to the age group of Wattpad's users, but I'm uncertain which platform received the most traffic from the dual ad. Nonetheless, I'm still analyzing data to plan my future marketing strategies for both Facebook and Instagram.

If you've published a book on Amazon's KDP site, you have the option of running low-cost campaigns that display in the carousel at the bottom of product pages. These ads have been more successful for me because Amazon's algorithms use your book's information to show your ads to visitors who are already browsing similar content and are more likely to be interested in your book. For beginners, I highly recommend this option as the impressions are higher and the cost per view is lower than Facebook's. Additionally, Amazon sells books, so the readers are already on the site.

Another marketing resource I have used is paying to be featured on book clubs' mailing lists. Some book clubs charge as little as $20 a day, while larger clubs charge over $200. Some authors swear by these mailing lists, but unfortunately, I didn't get a return on my investment.

Blog tours are a popular way to promote your book by connecting with a network of book bloggers. Essentially, you provide the tour organizer with links to your book, a pitch, a blurb, and images of both your book and yourself as an author. The organizer then pitches your book to their blogger connections, who decide whether or not to feature your book on their blog. I've had success with this method, although it does require some upfront effort. Ultimately, your book gets featured across multiple reader blogs, which can be a great way to get your work in front of more readers.

Paid marketing is another option, but it can be a tricky business. There are many factors to consider, and it often takes some trial and error to figure out what works best for your particular book.

Chapter 22
Moving on when something doesn't work

The definition of insanity is often stated as doing the same thing repeatedly and expecting different results. It's important to recognize that what works for one person may not work for another. For instance, while some authors have seen success with coupon promotions, it didn't yield the desired results for me. However, it's crucial to keep an open mind and give new methods a fair try for a few months. This allows you to evaluate visibility, analytics, and identify areas for improvement.

It's also essential to be true to yourself and focus on activities that bring you joy. If you have a passion for arts and crafts, consider creating swag to promote your work. This approach not only allows you to invest time in something you love, but also enables you to learn and promote your work effectively. Ultimately, your efforts should align with your interests, and it's vital to have patience and persistence to see results.

I have experience creating various types of advertisements, including online posters, a movie trailer, paid marketing advertisements, and marketing swag. Along with writing, I have a passion for photography, drawing, and design. Since childhood, I have kept a sketchbook and have always appreciated captivating visuals.

For the online posters I designed, I combined my own photos with concise messages to grab viewers' attention and promote the book I was advertising. This required me to utilize my writing, photography, and design skills to their fullest potential. I honed my photography skills by capturing and editing images in Photoshop to create multiple variations of the same photo. Then, I layered the images with short, compelling text to encourage viewers to read the novel.

To promote my book, I utilized social media platforms such as Facebook, Twitter, Pinterest, and my blog by posting digital posters. Rather than printing the images on paper, I decided to use them exclusively online.

To create paid advertisements, I followed templates provided by Goodreads and Facebook. Both platforms allowed for targeted audience selection and provided analytics to track the reach of the ads.

Goodreads offered a template that required a brief book description with a limited character count, a link to the book, and a book cover image. In contrast, Facebook's template was more flexible, allowing for the inclusion of images, videos, links, calls to action, and more text.

Despite seeing a fair amount of reach, I did not observe a significant increase in sales between paid and free advertisements.

I pursued the above activities driven by my personal interest, but I understand they may not be for everyone. For instance, if you dislike being on camera or taking videos, then there's no need to force yourself. Many successful authors do not have public social media profiles and some even outsource their editing. In case you have a hard "no" on something, it's completely acceptable to avoid it. If you force yourself to do something you hate, the outcome might reflect a lack of effort and time investment, which could damage your work. Hence, it's better to focus on what you enjoy and move   forward.

Chapter 23
Finding time for the other things that you love besides writing

When a new idea, scene, or character conversation pops up in your head, it's tempting to drop everything and start writing. But while inspiration can strike at any moment, it's important to find a balance between writing and other activities that bring you joy.

To avoid losing a great idea when you're short on time, jot down a few key sentences to summarize it for later use. And when you set aside time for writing but find yourself staring at a blank screen, it may be time to re-evaluate your schedule. Step away from the computer and focus on something else for a while. By finding a healthy balance between writing and other activities, you'll be more productive and inspired in the long run.

If you're determined to stick to your writing schedule, consider doing something productive to aid your writing process. For instance, you could proofread a previous chapter, work on your author profiles on social media, or improve your online marketing campaigns. However, it's essential to remember that your life is not solely about work. Once your scheduled writing time is up, take a break from your desk and laptop, and focus on self-care, rest, spending quality time with your loved ones, and being present in the moment.

Your writing will wait, and when you are ready, it will be exactly how you left it. It won't be sad that you left it alone. It won't judge you for focusing on other things. It won't punish you for failing to get one thousand words written in one sitting.

Be kind to yourself and allow yourself time and your writing will thank you.

About the Author

Carolynne Raymond is an Ottawa-area based author who writes science fiction, fantasy, and children's fiction. When she's not crafting tales, she enjoys reading, painting, and spending quality time with her husband and son.

Connect with Carolynne on:

Twitter: @cshaylo
Facebook: http://www.facebook.com/cshaylo
Instagram: carolynne.raymond
TikTok: @carolynneraymond

What is Next

More novels. I am writing the third and final novel to The Earth & Airus Series, my science-fiction series, wrapping up Taylan (Robin) and Kyle (Sitrus) stories.

www.ingramcontent.com/pod-product-compliance
Lightning Source LLC
Chambersburg PA
CBHW060338050426
42449CB00011B/2788